When your Child Divorces You

Estrangement

From Absalom to the Prodigal

Son

By

Jean Lash

Our youngest son said it would be 10 years before she would talk to us again.

Our pastor said he's heard of 30 years before reconciliation.

Other parents told me stories of 2, 4, 6 years before communication began again.

One rebellious young mom (in the church) told me it had been 6 years since she talked with her mom or dad.

Still other parents were waiting….hearing reports of their adult child doing drugs, living with "significant others", marrying, having children, moving overseas.

Another report was at 40 years. The mom finally passed away. The adult daughter contacted her dad just months before he, himself died.

Estrangement.

That ugly, embarrassing word that no one wants to talk about.

It screams failure.

Epic failure.

It can be between siblings (and usually is).

Or it can be with adult child and parents. There is a marked uptick in estrangement in this area. https://www.aarp.org/relationships/friends-family/info-03-2012/the-stranger-in-your-family.html

While it is easy to say "Epic fail!" with regard to estrangement….the Bible says otherwise.

God knew that estrangement would occur. He knew that as young people matured, there would be temptation to "break" with family.

He provided two examples in the Bible for us to follow. Two stories to ponder.

Page 4

I've learned a lot since our daughter, Sarah, broke from us,….now three years ago.

While we miss her terribly, we realize there is a plan…put in place for her, and for us.

We are not "left alone" to consider and re-consider "what went wrong".

We are not to live in a state of constant "re-hashing" of the events that led up to the estrangement.

Rather we are to follow the examples set before us in Scripture.

God has purposed this time in both her life and ours.

As painful as it has been for us…. there has been light and good, come out in the darkness of estrangement.

I wrote this book to help others, as they "wait" on their prodigal child.

TABLE OF CONTENTS

It is not uncommon for youth and young adults to want to "go their own way".

It is an age-old story.

It almost always has an exciting beginning, a shocking middle, and a sad ending.

Especially for young women who go forward without their family's blessing.

I am the child of a rebellious young woman who grew up in the 1960's. I am her only child. I was the toddler, whose mom divorced (my dad), my dad lost custody, ... and as a result, I never knew my dad.

Conversely, there are those youth and young people who truly love and enjoy their family.

These have learned to cherish their biological family, and still venture forth to build their own lives.

They seem to have found that "balance" of love, affection, honor, duty....and setting their own path....simultaneously.

One of the hardest questions posed in this life is: what makes a young person disdain.... hate............ stop talking to his parents?

Chapter 1

The Good, 'Ole Days

Each of us parents remembers those sweet days....holding our newborn, changing

her diapers, showing her to family and friends. As she grew, the mornings she

jumped into bed with her siblings and yourself. We remember the first time she

read a book, rode a bike and planted a flower.

We have drawers of cards and pictures and small little gifts,....from small little

hands.

Never in a million years did we think he could stop talking to us. Hate us. Disdain

us.

He said a million times, "Mama, Daddy...I love you".

Why doesn't he love us now?

First, we must cherish those times. Those sweet times that we remember were

a gift. A gift from God. Precious. We must be thankful and grateful for those

years.

No healing for ourselves can begin....without being thankful for the good times.

Many people have stillborn children, disabled children, or children that die within a few hours, or a few years of birth.

We, at least, had a fair amount of good times with our child. That must be recognized and appreciated.

We must be thankful for all those times we had. That is one area of our focus.

Ask yourself: How thankful am I for the good memories?

It can be a sweet relief (from the current reality) to thumb through old pictures and notes and videos of those days.

It can also be painfully hard to realize the vast chasm that now lies before us.

If you find yourself extremely sad over your estranged child, it is NOT the time to look through the old photos. This activity can plunge you into an almost immovable depression.

If you find yourself feeling grateful and happy, it is the time to dwell on those things.

Secondly, we need to come to grips that our child will have his own story.

His current choices will have consequences.

Her decision to sever ties with you, will have consequences.

God is working and moving in his life.

Yes, I know. You cannot see it.

I can't either....most of the time.

But that doesn't mean that God is not acting on my child.

He is.

God is slow to anger and abounding in patience.

We are not.

Thus, He is working on us too.

Ask yourself: Can I allow God to "work on my child", separate from me?

Do I believe there is 'other' good that can come of this? Helping someone else through it, being more empathetic when I hear of estragement/rebellion, etc?

Chap 2

What Happened?.....Lessons from Absalom & the Prodigal Son

So many people ask us estranged parents: "So what happened?" "Why doesn't

Jimmy (or Susie) talk to you anymore?"

What a loaded question.

It isn't easy to answer.

And the answers are as varied as the day is long.

The short answer is: slowly Jimmy changed.

Each parent's story will be different.

But all of our stories will have some "common denominators".

Here goes....

For all of us, Jimmy (or Susie) went from loving us in his younger years....to slowly

disagreeing with our worldview and/or the decisions we were making.

Over time, Jimmy met up with others who shared his new perspective.

(Or gave him an entirely new one/equally as bad.)

Either way, Jimmy "broke" with our worldview....first, in his mind, then with his friends, and finally physically "broke" the relationship with us.

Good, bad or indifferent...that is the general progression of estrangement.

Jimmy reasoned (and continues to reason) that it is better **not** to reconcile ....than **to** reconcile with his family.

Jimmy has "done the math", and either: is too hurt, reconciling is too hard, too troubling, won't change things, or Jimmy feels affirmed apart from his parents.

This is the pattern of estrangement.

You, as the parent, also feel hurt, betrayed, troubled, ...but you have the longer, greater perspective, and desire to reconcile in some fashion.

The key to this disconnect is: youth..., young people...., young adults.

Estrangement almost always occurs in someone's youth. Rarely is the person over 30 years old.

Young people feel they have all the answers, many years before them, things to do, places to go, and time on their side. Youth know that you "just might" want the relationship more than they do (at least right now).

This is the story of both Absalom and the prodigal son.

They are in different parts of the Bible….Absalom in the Old Testament and the prodigal son in the New Testament.

There are similarities, differences, and a TON of lessons to learn in these stories.

1. Both of these are young men, in their youth, without perspective

2. Both have a desire to do something separate and different from their parent

3. Both dishonor and sin against their parent

4. Both have opportunities/chances to redeem the situation…only one does

5. God works on both young men

6. Both fathers grieve

7. There are consequences for both young men

I like to think of estrangement as falling into one of two categories.

One category: the parent's choices/issues/sin ushered in the estrangement.

The second category: the young person brought on the estrangement.

The David/Absalom estrangement falls into the first category...David's choices had the unintended consequence of estrangement with his son.

Conversely, the prodigal son is the main "actor"...bringing estrangement to the relationship.

Let's start with Absalom.

Chap 3   The David/Absalom Estrangement

After King David commits adultery with Bathsheba...David has her husband Uriah killed, and then takes Bathsheba as one of his wives.

When Nathan, God's prophet comes to rebuke David...David confesses his sin against God.

Consequences, however, are in order, and Nathan says the following:

Now therefore, the sword shall never depart from your house, because you have despised Me and have taken the wife of Uriah the Hittite to be your wife.' 11 "Thus says the LORD, 'Behold, I will raise up evil against you from your own household; I will even take your wives before your eyes and give *them* to your companion, and he will lie with your wives in broad daylight. 12 'Indeed you did it secretly, but I will do this thing before all Israel, and under the sun.'"

There is so much in the above verses in 2 Sam 12. God calls down judgement/consequences for David, and says he will do them BECAUSE DAVID DESPISED HIM (the Lord). The sins David committed were boiled down to:

Despising the Lord.

When we don't do what is right....we are actually despising the Lord.

After this time in David's life, his family begins to go downhill, just as the Lord had said. One of his son's rapes his half-sister. His other son, Absalom, kills the rapist-son. Over time, David and Absalom become estranged, and eventually Absalom betrays his father, and usurps the throne.

 I've often thought, "Is my estranged daughter, Sarah…., an "Absalom"?

Is the David/Absalom story…… my story?

Or does our story fall into the prodigal son story?

I have read and re-read the story in 1 Sam 12….and looked carefully at the details.

What had preceded the David/Absalom estrangement?

1. David looking at others   (think lust/pornography)

2. David sleeping with others.

3. David plotting, then killing, another human being.

4. Sexual sin in David's home,…1/2 brother/sister

5. David's reluctance to act regarding his young people's sexual sin

6. David's seeming indifference to the rape of his daughter

As I tick through this list, I don't see any similarities in my personal situation with my daughter.   But other estranged parents do.

How do these points translate to current situations of estrangement?

Questions to ask when dealing with your estrangement...

Was there pornography in the family prior to the estrangement with your child?

Was there another relationship, or fornication, or adultery in the family or home?

Was there some kind of sexual sin in your home prior to estrangement?

Have serious sins been committed in your home that, have been "swept under the rug?" (Not everyday parental mistakes and errors.)

Were you, or the other parent, reluctant to act on serious matters?

Were you, or the other parent, indifferent to the physical abuse of a child?

Was a loved one in the family (child, elderly member) "not taken care of"?

Neglected? "Farmed out to others" for daily care? A young child? A teenager?

An older relative?

Was a relative raped, abused, violently attacked or molested, under your care?

The young person can feel very "jarred" to say the least, at any of the above. Their worldview can begin to take a different course, and change direction…with the above serious issues.

Absalom most likely, was aware of David's sin with Bathsheba. The very fact that David liked/loved multiple women, was probably a big problem for Absalom growing up. Absalom may have yearned for a more nuclear family life, but instead had many half- brothers, and half- sisters.

David reaction (or inaction) with regard to Absalom's sister's rape was extremely troubling to Absalom. Seeking justice for his sister was his new role.

After Absalom killed his half-brother in revenge, he skipped town for quite a while. The estrangement began. David struggled finding a "way back" with Absalom, and never seemed to take the steps to re-connect with him.

We see the typical progression of estrangement:

Absalom begins to break (within himself) with David. Then, Absalom's "break" moved to his circle of friends. Finally he completely broke with David.

For those of us who have experienced it, the young person can also plot, plan, betray, and slander their parents.

Absalom did it all. Planned quietly and carefully his moves. Manipulated situations and people to get where he wanted. Betrayed his father. Abandoned "natural" loyalty. Began to slander and twist the truth.

Absalom took over the kingdom for a time…while his father David ran.

Can you imagine David's grief? It is one thing to run from your enemy.

It is quite another to run from your child… who has turned into your enemy.

We all know the story of God's final judgement on Absalom: while riding horseback, his long hair catches in a tree. It hangs him and another man kills him.

Though David cried, "Oh, Absalom, Oh, Absalom…my son, my son!" at Absalom's death….everyone else had watched the betrayal of son to father.

Everyone else in the story seemed to welcome a defeated Absalom.

So David grieved alone.

David remembered the sweet infant boy of days gone by, that used to love him.

When I was a little girl, reading this story…I never understood why David was sad

to lose Absalom….wasn't David happy not to be on the run anymore?

Wasn't he glad…that Absalom had been totally defeated?

Now that my own child has done similar things….

Now I know, all too well….those sweet memories David was recalling.

The love of a parent for a child defies all logic. The bonds of parent for child are

great and strong….I think, much stronger than the child for the parent.

David's story is extreme.

Probably none of us will have an estranged child try to take our position at our

workplace…, or hunt us down…like Absalom did David.

But we may have a child slander us, betray us, feel no honor/duty toward us.

Sniff at our worldview.

Laugh at our interests.

Mock our positions.

We taste a "bit" of what David tasted…and we mourn like David mourned.

Takeaways from David/Absalom:

1. Absalom is not let "off the hook" by God. Even though David's sin had serious consequences, Absalom continued to dishonor his father. Multiple times. We never see him repent toward David. God allows small victories for Absalom, but David ultimately wins the war....Absalom has a crashing bitter end.

2. While God forgives us parents for what preceded the estrangement, we still must face the consequences, in the case of serious sin: other relationships, sexual sin, abandonment, neglect, physical abuse, etc.

3. The best thing for the parent to do is confess their fault to the adult child. Own what you did. Ask for forgiveness. Figure out and try to "make a way" for reconciliation. To do less than this, puts you in a precarious position. The position David found himself in.

4. No one, absolutely no one....can take away our sweet memories of our estranged child.

4. No one can take away the love we remember for our estranged child.

This fierce/illogical love can both serve us, and be our defeat. It is a natural, God-given blessing to love our child (even more) than they love us. It provokes us to pray for them (when we'd rather not).

But it can also plunge us into the deepest depressions of loss and grief.

It can cause us not to appreciate those who ARE STICKING AROUND....and loving us daily.

In the story, general Joab almost had to slug David ....to get David to see and appreciate those who had helped him run from Absalom.

May that never be said of us...... as we grieve, wait, hope, and pray for our child.

Chap 4

What Good can Come from any kind of Estrangement?

Another loaded question.

My only feeble answer is: looking at everything in a new light.

Maybe this happened to remind each of us: it really is just the Lord and myself...at the end of the day.

Maybe this isn't "about me".

Maybe "it's not about us".

Maybe this happened to help others....somehow.

Obviously, David became closer to the Lord throughout all of these events.

Have we clung to the Lord, in this, our desperate hour?

Are we finding ways to help others with their wayward child?

It is completely normal/natural to be raw, and in shock, as your child pulls away and out of your life.

They've been in your life upwards of two decades...and now...poof! They're gone.

I liken it much to a death.

And we know death has shock, denial, grief, and healing.

Don't expect to do much helping at the beginning.

In the beginning you cry.

You slowly, ever so slowly, begin to accept what is happening.

All the help I could give at that time (for others seeking help) was commiseration and prayer on behalf of their wayward child. I did manage to say to one couple, "You guys did a great job raising _____. I saw it myself for almost 10 years….please don't blame yourselves." After I said that, it felt really good….like maybe God had used me, as a sweet-smelling balm for that hurting couple.

Grief is the next step….where weeks go by and you remember: every little thing from their infancy and childhood….every sweet time together. The memories flood in like a storm. And the reality you hold in one hand (no contact/estrangement) and your memories keep trying to "mesh" in your brain…but they don't.

Slowly, ever so slowly….there is a new normal. Holidays pass. Birthdays. Events where your child was always present….but she is no longer.

You begin to accept the new normal. It doesn't hurt as bad as it used to.

Now you are stronger.

Now you can truly help.

I have more compassion toward other parents that have a struggling child.

I have more understanding for families where a young adult chooses poorly.

I have more empathy for moms and dads who were fooled or manipulated.

I listen more readily…understand more deeply….and grieve alongside.

God has brought me many families with similar pain….and I can help.

I remind myself over and over that my chief end is my relationship with God, ….not with my child.

My whole purpose is to glorify God, ….not a relationship with my child.

I seem to notice (more) the young adults around me: at the grocery store, in the church, in the community. I've learned to step out of my comfort zone and talk to, and befriend.....those that seem hurting or lost.

I'm braver.

I don't care if it's odd to reach out to strangers.

I've lost a child.

What do I have to lose?

Maybe I can encourage them back in the right direction. And maybe back in a good relationship with their families.

I try not to think of my personal loss of my daughter as much.

Instead, I try and replace the loss with: who has God put in front of me right now? What is He asking me to do, right now?

This estrangement didn't happen to you for nothing.

Ask yourself: What does God want me to do with it?

Chap 5

The Prodigal Son

Hope for the Hopeless

My hope for you is that you have a prodigal son or daughter.

One who, in the rush of youth, has acted foolishly and carelessly.

One that will eventually come back to you.

Not one that is estranged forever, like Absalom.

Jesus' story of the prodigal is probably one of the most beloved in the Bible. The story has overtones of our Heavenly Father waiting patiently for us.

But the story also has intricate details of estrangement between a parent and child.

Details that we must not miss.

Details that will be our guide...in our current estrangement.

Here's the passage...it has so much to offer the estranged parent....

Luke 15:11-32 King James Version (KJV)

11 And he said, A certain man had two sons:

12 And the younger of them said to his father, Father, give me the portion of goods that falleth to me. And he divided unto them his living.

13 And not many days after the younger son gathered all together, and took his journey into a far country, and there wasted his substance with riotous living.

14 And when he had spent all, there arose a mighty famine in that land; and he began to be in want.

15 And he went and joined himself to a citizen of that country; and he sent him into his fields to feed swine.

16 And he would fain have filled his belly with the husks that the swine did eat: and no man gave unto him.

17 And when he came to himself, he said, How many hired servants of my father's have bread enough and to spare, and I perish with hunger!

18 I will arise and go to my father, and will say unto him, Father, I have sinned against heaven, and before thee,

19 And am no more worthy to be called thy son: make me as one of thy hired servants.

20 And he arose, and came to his father. But when he was yet a great way off, his father saw him, and had compassion, and ran, and fell on his neck, and kissed him.

21 And the son said unto him, Father, I have sinned against heaven, and in thy sight, and am no more worthy to be called thy son.

22 But the father said to his servants, Bring forth the best robe, and put it on him; and put a ring on his hand, and shoes on his feet:

²³ And bring hither the fatted calf, and kill it; and let us eat, and be merry:

²⁴ For this my son was dead, and is alive again; he was lost, and is found. And they began to be merry.

²⁵ Now his elder son was in the field: and as he came and drew nigh to the house, he heard musick and dancing.

²⁶ And he called one of the servants, and asked what these things meant.

²⁷ And he said unto him, Thy brother is come; and thy father hath killed the fatted calf, because he hath received him safe and sound.

²⁸ And he was angry, and would not go in: therefore came his father out, and intreated him.

²⁹ And he answering said to his father, Lo, these many years do I serve thee, neither transgressed I at any time thy commandment: and yet thou never gavest me a kid, that I might make merry with my friends:

³⁰ But as soon as this thy son was come, which hath devoured thy living with harlots, thou hast killed for him the fatted calf.

³¹ And he said unto him, Son, thou art ever with me, and all that I have is thine.

³² It was meet that we should make merry, and be glad: for this thy brother was dead, and is alive again; and was lost, and is found.

1. Note there are two sons. This will have significance in the total family

estrangement,....as **there will be issues between the sons as well.**

2. The Bible does not fault the parent/father in any way.

Surely the father had made mistakes and errors in bringing up his boys. Yet, there is no mention of serious sin in this family.

3. We assume that the prodigal son is in his youth. It is possible that he is middle aged, but certainly not "old".

4. The Bible does not tell us "why" the son wants to leave. Perhaps it is because it doesn't matter why. Perhaps it is because any reasons (short of serious sins/talked about earlier) don't "count" in God's book. So Jesus did not include the "reasons". For the record, typical youth complaints are: "You raised me wrong", "You made me mad", "You yelled at me", "I don't like the way you handled things," etc.... God is not interested in these complaints. God allows for mistakes and errors in parenting.

5. The son dishonors his father and asks for his "part" of the inheritance/finances/money....long before the time.

6. Not only that... he wants to leave the family and travel to a far-off area....he wants to go where it will be nearly impossible for the father to know his well-being.

7. He wants to shirk his family responsibilities. What responsibilities? Responsibilities of his part of the work, duty to look after his father...physically and emotionally, ...any duties toward his brother. Duties to be kind and civil, decent, communicative, and affectionate. The younger son is "done" with the family and the family lifestyle. His actions make a mockery of "Honor your father and mother."

8. The younger son wants/takes valuable family assets...that others have worked for/had in their possession..... He would "receive" his father's assets...without reciprocating. **He wastes them, with riotous living.** **He spends it all.**

I want to stop here and bring up a few things:

9. Much time passes. We are not told how much time. We do not have a definite time frame. Perhaps it is intentionally left out. Maybe, because for you...it will be 3 years, ...and for me, it will be 10. For someone else it will be 25 years. Jesus' story fits "all" of our estranged parents stories. There's a song called "God is in the waiting". There is much truth in that statement.

10. The father/parent is in the dark. No communication that we are told of. **The younger son has gone "cold and dark".**

11. The father/parent does not hunt him down. He does not search him out. Figure out where he is. Send some of his servants to spy on him. The father does not beg him to return/reconcile. He does not send letters of apology or connection.

12. During this time, the other son is dutifully working. Providing physical and emotional support. Picking up the pieces of younger brother's mess.

13. The father keeps a good relationship with those that love him... we see near the end of the story that the older son/father can speak frankly and sincerely with each other. They have had good fellowship during this trial. The father has obviously treated his servants/employees well, as they dutifully obey him throughout the story.....it can't be stressed enough to LOVE THE ONES THAT ARE LOVING YOU BACK (be it friends, family, co-workers)....don't take out your grief on them....

14. God is working....long before the father knows anything.....God has a plan for the son....first He sends a famine....then the son begins to be in want, ...then he joins himself/works for someone in that country….feeding pigs…..down to hardly anything….

15. The son: comes to himself, thinks about home, wants to go back… this is the wonderful moment that all of us estranged parents are waiting for….

I want you to stop again.

Look at what the son goes through….how many signs from God….that he is on the wrong path….BEFORE he actually gets it.

You could call it hard head, stubborn will, so full of himself!

THIS IS OUR GUIDE…..

Estranged parent: this is the process.

This is how long it takes.

This is what the child has to go through.

But it gets better.

16. The son repents toward God first, and parent second. Just like David, the sin is against God first.

17. The son realizes (maybe for the first time) the value of his family/parent. The son "practices" what he will say in order, just to live...on the property....as a servant.

18. The son realizes he doesn't deserve to be called a son or family member. The son (rightfully) acknowledges that there are consequences to what he has done.

Now, we turn to the parent.

19. God prepares the father/parent. The father "sees the son a long way off". Interesting. Why was he looking a long way off, that day? After so many days of no contact? I can only think that God has begun the work of preparing the father. God had the father look that particular day.... God had planted the seeds of reconciliation in the father's heart.

20. The father had compassion, ran, showed affection. Any hurt, anger, bitterness, and resentment were already put aside. The very sight of the son moved the father. The father had no words of disappointment or disapproval.

21. The father treats the son like a VIP….new clothes, shoes, ring, party…..his actions show that he has completely forgiven the son and wants to reconcile.

STOP AGAIN.

When the reconciling actually happens to us someday…it is NOT the time to discuss the past.

It is not the time to reveal the hurts you've been carrying around for years.

It's possible that time will come later. But not now.

22. The older son hears that younger brother is home. Remember, that they are siblings. This is not the "fierce love" of a parent. The normal sibling rivalry has most likely turned to disgust and disdain, in the older son's eyes. He is not thrilled, thankful, overjoyed. He has been carrying the burden of making the father "as happy as he could" all these years. Then here, comes Johnny....having

spent all dad's money....currently whooping it up at a party.

23. The older son's anger vents to the top....he refuses to go in. The father has a

"new" problem...with the other son, now. The older son is finally free to speak

what he really thinks... "I served thee ....I didn't transgress....you gave me no

party...YOUR SON has come home....he devoured your money with harlots...."

We should expect our other children and family members to be angry, resentful,

and disgusted with, our estranged child. They do not have the fierce love of a

parent. They see the grave injustice.

**24. The father immediately redeems the situation: "Thou art ever with me and

all that I have is thine".....**the father wisely differentiates the relationships....he

admits that he and the older son have a special/different kind of relationship. It is

a "given" that all the assets of the fathers' are his.....he reminds the son that "We

should make merry....he was dead and is alive."

What a wonderful story! I pray and hope for that story in your life. I hope and pray for it in my life. Every time I read it, I am encouraged with regard to my Sarah. I know that this is God's way.

It may not be what your friends are telling you.

It may not be what your co-workers are telling you.

It may be what the extended family is telling you.

It may not be what your church is telling you.

But this is what God is telling you.

He didn't leave us without a story, ...to be our guide.

God has shown you the path.

He's not left you without a way.

God is in the waiting.

Chap 6

What to do While you Wait

Something.

Anything.

It will be a while.

What comes to your mind?....when you hear the words, "What should I do, while I wait?"

What you hear is probably God's advice to you.

Believe it or not, you are not just a parent.

You are a living, breathing human being with interests, skills, and gifting.

Since you have to wait,.....what else would you like to do with you life in the meantime?

You are a useful, valuable person with much to give.

You will feel better emotionally, and be better physically, if you follow where God is leading.

What else would you like to do, before you die?

What can you put your mind on, and your back into?

God will bless you...for letting Him work on your child.

He knows how much you miss him.

He knows how much it hurts.

The work that God has to do in your child's life...takes time.

It is not done (well) quickly.

To hasten God's work, would only benefit you...and not your child.

It must be complete, step-by-step change in your child's heart.

Your child must think and reflect. Compare and contrast. The "old way" he used to know; and the results of the "new path" he has chosen.

Meantime, your energies are best placed somewhere else.

Chap 7

Honor your Father and Mother

After God hands out the 10 commandments, we notice that the first four are about Him. The commandments following are about others.

The first one (about others) is Father and Mother.

Honor your Father and Mother.

It's clear language.

It doesn't say you have to obey them the rest of your life (after you're grown).

It says honor.

Respect.

Work with.

Give.

Compromise.

Take into consideration.

Thus, at any age (18, 38, 58, etc)…we are to try hard to honor our parents.

If something seriously displeases them, we do our best to "see" if we can arrange things in that favor.

They may not be 100% happy with the outcome, but we are to try.

We can even get to the point of "agreeing to disagree", but with otherwise good fellowship, love and affection.

This will take a tremendous amount of energy.

Lots of conversations.

Honest talking.

Pouring out of one's heart.

Offering of multiple options.

The lines of communication are to never totally break down.

Take note that the commandment is to the child.

No matter what age.

The "onus" is on the child. It is not on the parent.

The commandment is not: Honor your child.

Too many in society read the parent-adult child relationship that way.

God chose this particular commandment as the first in a series of commandments dealing with other people...not Himself.

Parents are the first and primary relationship an individual has.

The other commandments go on to talk about spouses, neighbors, and people in general.

But parents are first.

God was not haphazard in ordering these commandments.

Perhaps He knew our tendency to kinda "sweep the parents" away from time to time.

Our lives will never be complete ... without honestly trying as hard as possible to honor our parents, while working out disagreements and differences.

Ultimately, we are to keep contact, love and affection...no matter our life choices.

The commandment is to any child (no matter the age) with a living parent.

You will be blessed for your efforts at honoring your parents.

The Bible uses the language....."that it may be well with thee and thou mayest live long on the earth". (Eph 6:3)..

While the Old Testament gives us the initial commandment "Honor thy father and thy mother....the New Testament ...here in Ephesians adds..."that it my be well with thee"....

My own mother did not honor her family's wishes in her marriage to my dad.

I can testify for a fact that "it did not go well" for her.

Our current situation of our children "divorcing us" and not honoring us sets the stage.

It sets the stage of things "not going well" for them....sometime in the future.

While that is a sad thought (added to our grief) it is a promise.

It did not go well for Absalom.

One could even argue that in parts of the prodigal son's life...it did not go well. He did have what he could have had. He didn't experience what he could have experienced.

Afterword

God is in the Business of Second Chances

If you have been involved in serious sins, like David, and have been estranged

from your child...God will give you a second chance.

Likewise, if your child has chosen poorly in his youth....God will give him a second

chance as well.

God works with us broken people. He knows our failings. He loves us with a

reckless love...nonetheless.

I decided to write this book, when I saw so little help for estranged parents. No

one would talk about it, in the terms God does.

Also, it was disturbing to see the suicidal issues estranged parents face....I wanted

to provide hope and help....during this time of grief.

I hope it has been a comfort to you. God is in the waiting. jeannelash@aol.com

Made in the USA
Coppell, TX
01 November 2022

85609245R00025